Billy and Me
and a
Cowboy in Black
and other poems

Eric Finney

Pictures by Sue Heap

Edward Arnold

© Eric Finney 1986
Illustrations © Sue Heap 1986

First published in Great Britain 1986 by
Edward Arnold (Publishers) Ltd
41 Bedford Square, London WC1B 3DQ

Edward Arnold (Australia) Pty Ltd
80 Waverley Road, Caulfield East
Victoria 3145, Australia

British Cataloguing in Publication Data

Finney, Eric
Billy and me and a cowboy in black.—(Billy and me)
  I. Title   II. Heap, Sue
  821'.914   PR6056.I518/

ISBN 0–7131–7394–7

Riddles
Tadpole
Grandfather, son, grandson
Coffin
Planet Earth

Text set in 12/15pt Century
by The Castlefield Press, Moulton, Northampton
Printed in Great Britain by Butler & Tanner Ltd, Frome, Somerset
and bound by W H Ware and Sons Ltd, Clevedon, Avon

Contents

Billy and Me and a Cowboy in Black

I told you about that igloo we built
And how it shrank a bit each day –
Well, it wasn't long after the last hump of snow
Had finally melted away
That Sir said, "You all know
About Help the Aged:
Well, I'm on the committee,
And we're organising a sponsored walk
To raise some cash. It's a pity
That all of you are so unfit and that
You've forgotten how to walk . . ."
Just the kind of remark our teacher makes
To raise a storm of talk.
When that'd died down our Billy said,
"Why d'you say walking's forgotten?"
And Sir said, "It's true –
When it comes to transport
You're all of you just spoilt rotten:
You get brought to school and picked up
By car,
You expect buses door to door;
You'd never do this sponsored walk –
You've forgotten what legs are for."
"How far is it, Sir?"
"Are you doing it, Sir?"
"Are you taking your trouble and strife?"
"It's twenty miles and yes, I am going,
And all being well, so's my wife."
Billy says, "Ah now, if your wife's going
I think I'd better be there . . ."
Billy's a bit sweet on our teacher's wife –

She's pretty with long blonde hair;
She's got blue eyes as well, a lovely soft voice,
And a smile like the sun breaking through –
Billy reckons he might have married her himself
If Sir hadn't been first in the queue.
"Anyway," says Sir, "just give it some thought.
Of course, you'd need parents' permission.
It's a bit of a challenge, a stamina test,
A trial, an adventurous mission.
Think of Tensing and Hilary, Everest men;
Think of Scott exploring the Pole;
Think of Livingstone's quest for the source of the Nile –
This is only a twenty mile stroll!"
He gets carried away sometimes does Sir –
Still, I got in a sly word or two:
"Think of sore feet and blisters, exhaustion
And cramp, getting fed up, or scorched,
Or wet through."

On the way home I said to Billy,
"You're not going to really do it?"
"Why not?" says Billy, "we'll do it together –
Twenty miles man – there's nothing to it.
Besides, if you think, it's a pretty good cause:
We might manage to raise a few quid;
After all, it's quite possible one day, you know,
We'll be old and need helping out, kid."

"You pair walk twenty miles!" said Dad,
"Excuse my hysterical mirth!"
"Never mind laughing," our Billy said,
"If we do it, what's it worth?"
"But you hardly walk anywhere ever," said Dad,
"You like cars, buses, bikes and armchairs –
You'd get on your bikes to go to the loo
If the smallest room wasn't upstairs!

I'll tell you what, though,
If you finish the course –
And it's up on the hills where it's bleak –
When I'm over the shock, there's a fiver apiece
And I'll give up my beer for a week!"

It started from school on a cold April Saturday –
Rangers at home, worse luck;
We'd got waterproofs, rucksacks and all the right gear:
Dad'd borrowed things when we got stuck.
Mum'd put up the grub – enough for a dozen –
Soup, sandwiches, fruit, all packed neat;
We gave our names in at the desk and got numbers
Then we started off pounding our feet.

There were only a few kids from school going walkies
But among them, amazing to say,
Was fat Reggie Bestwick – the last kid on earth
I'd have thought would be walking that day.
He's always in trouble with teachers is Reggie,
Being cheeky or having a fight;
Our Dad says he's seen him down town
In the back streets,
Just roaming about late at night.
Reggie as usual is all dressed in black –
Black trousers, black sweater, black shirt:
Says he's ready for funerals if they turn up,
Besides that, it don't show the dirt.
He got the idea from this Western on telly
With a gunfighter dressed in black gear,
And Reggie today's got a crummy black stetson,
Black wellies, a black ring in one ear.
He keeps pretty cheerful in spite of the trouble,
He's a bit of a pal of our Bill,
So we walked along with him a bit,
Then we left him
Still puffing his way up Long Hill.

8

There's this mad twisty road to the top of Long Hill
With a steep rocky drop off the side,
And there's all kinds of bits of old cars
In the bottom –
Your car hits some ice and you slide.
Then it's flat sandy tracks
For four or five miles
With oceans of bilberry and heather,
And there's Billy and me, with the wind on our backs,
Just striding it out together.
We passed a few folks, but no one passed us –
I tell you, I've never felt fitter –
And Billy said, "Hey, what's the betting
That Sir's up ahead at the pub
Drinking bitter?"

9

We came down off the hill
With the wind blowing keen
And the hang-gliders drifting like hawks,
To the pub – it was called
The Labour in Vain –
Our Billy's eyes popping on stalks:
He's looking for Sir,
More especially his wife –
Billy fancies a bit of a gas –
And they're there drinking beer,
They buy us lemonade,
And we stretch ourselves out on the grass;
And there's everyone there –
Men, women and kids,
And they've taken off boots, socks and kit,
And they're scoffing their sandwiches,
Nursing their feet –
The sun's even shining a bit.
It was one of those times I'll remember for ever:
I couldn't say why, I just will –
Everyone happy and chatting and laughing
At the pub by the foot of Long Hill.

The
Labour
in
VAIN

But there's cloud rolling up
And the chill wind is back
And suddenly sunshine is gone;
We're not quite half-way
So I say to our Billy,
"Hey, sunbeam, we'd better get on."
As we went from the pub, there were two coming in,
The school team's left back and the goalie:
They'd got news of Reggie – a couple of miles back –
Still coming – extremely slowly.
Out to the Tallstones – my feet a bit sore now –
In the wind there's the sting of rain;
The half-way checkpoint; Billy says,
"Man, we've got this much to do again!"

The route back's a road
On Long Hill's other slope,
It's narrow with passing places;
Heather: plenty; shelter: none,
Wind and rain in our faces.
Heads down, all conversation gone,
The weather now really spiteful,
And a chap drives up – official car –
Leans out:
"Chaps, isn't it frightful!
You've done terribly well, but there's five miles yet –
Jump in, we'll be home in one!"
Billy looks at me, and I give him the nod:
"No thanks, pal, we're walking on.
I tell you what though: there is a hombre
Who'd be glad of a quick lift back –
A few miles down the way you're going
There's a soaking wet cowboy in black."
He gives us a bit of a look does this bloke
But drives on without any niggling,
And Billy and me pass the next mile or three
Remembering his face and giggling.
Maybe the rain's eased off a bit now –
It's just raining hard, not pouring;
We're both pretty wet in our waterproofs
And the last few miles are boring.
A lot of the walkers have taken lifts –
Out from car windows they peer;
We get lots of offers but we say, "No thanks,
We've got to get Dad off the beer!"

So we limp in at last
And there's loads of hot tea,
And we go to the desk where they list us
And give us certifs – then we take off our boots
To take a first look at our blisters.
It's nice hanging about and telling our tale
And seeing the folks come and go;
There's Sir – half an hour after us – and he calls,
"I salute you King Billy and Co!"
Then there's Dad with the car
To take us back home –
He's grinning from ear to ear:
You can see that he's pleased we finished the route
Though it's costing him money and beer.

"Hey, what about Reggie?" our Billy says.
There's nobody seen him for yonks,
But just then there's a car
Come back off the route
And the driver pulls in and honks.
"There's a cowboy in black 'bout a mile out of town,
He's staggering like somebody boozed;
He's plumb tuckered out –
I offered a lift
But he waved me away and refused."
"We'll give him an escort of honour!"
Shouts Billy,
"Come on everybody, get dressed!"
And twelve of us then
Ambled back up the road
To greet the Man of the West.
About half a mile back fat Reggie's still coming,
He's hobbling something cruel,
But his grin's still wide
And he's not too tired
To clown about and fool:
"Reggie hits town with his six guns blazing,
His strength and stamina are truly amazing!"
Sir offers him a beer bottle
And Reggie takes a slurp;
Rounds it all off
With a mighty burp.

Dad said as he drove us home,
"You both did well, I'd say."
"Yeh, pretty well," said Billy,
"But I reckon it's Reggie's day."

What I Did in the Summer Holiday

Oh, nothing much . .

Climbed Everest one afternoon,
Took a day trip to the moon,
For England scored a vital winner,
Took the Queen and Duke to dinner;

Won six Olympic gongs – all gold,
Found a cure for the common cold,
On five occasions topped the charts,
Transplanted half a dozen hearts;

Rowed the Nile from sea to source:
Against the current? But of course!
Read the news on BBC;
"Why not for us?" said ITV;

Outgunned Clint Eastwood in a Western,
Went to both Poles without a vest on,
Shot Niagara by canoe,
Biked from here to Timbuctoo;
Met Russia and the USA –
Got them to chuck their bombs away . . .

A pretty dull time as a rule;
I'm thankful to be back at school.

It's Different this Autumn

October's here and you'll never guess:
"We'll write about Autumn again," says Miss,
"And let's try and escape from the same old ruts –
No squirrels, please, hiding hoards of nuts
Or rustling of red and yellow leaves,
Or swallows twittering under eaves;
No cobwebs hung with beads of dew –
Do try to come up with something new.
I don't mind whether it's verse or prose."

Something different . . . well, here goes:

Off we trudge in our ballet shoes
On muddy Autumn tracks,
While leaves in shades of black and white
Clatter noisily down on our backs;

Along the lane the pineapples hang
And coconuts cling like confetti,
And here come the chaps with their harvest nets
To catch the ripe spaghetti.

Behind them, with his spaghetti gun,
Urging them ever faster,
Comes the expert, the number one
Master pasta blaster.
There, at the foot of yonder beech,
I'm sure it's a duck-billed platypus,
Lining her nest with barbed wire strands
To defend it against our tatty puss.

POLE WEST EAST SOUTH

And overhead the boa constrictors
In great flocks wheel and roll,
Migrating south or east or west
Or maybe up the Pole;
A tarantula swings from web to web
Scratching his hairy belly –
But now farewell, we must get home
To tea and toast and telly.

When she marked it, I don't think she noticed anything
    odd;
She wrote at the bottom (the way they do, thinking
    themselves like God):
"This is not as interesting as the piece you wrote last
    Friday.
Sentence construction poor – and why is it so untidy?"

20

Four Riddles

Head with a tail,
Each day plumper,
On the way
From jelly to jumper.

Two fathers and two sons
Went fishing from the beach;
Altogether caught three fishes,
And that was one fish each.
Does that sound rather odd to you?
Well, try it through again,
And when you think you've worked it out –
Explain.

Case
For last place.

Space Vehicle:
One of a fleet of nine.
This one, though,
Is yours and mine.

The Best Film Ever

Did you see that film on telly last night?
It nearly gave my Mum a fit,
Especially when that ghastly green horror
Came drooling and slobbering
Out of the pit.

And what about that bit where the vampire
Silently stalks the empty moat?
And climbs in at the bedroom window
Of this girl in the white nightie,
And sucks her throat.

There was one bit though, that I hardly dared watch,
'Cos I hate these things that slither:
It was when they hauled this giant squid up
From a thousand fathoms, and you saw
It die and wither.

And then that ginormous, grinning spider
Caught this explorer called Bruce,
And caged him inside his eight hairy legs,
And cocooned and paralysed him,
Then sucked his juice.

I've not even mentioned the Egyptian mummy,
Or Frankenstein, or the yeti;
Oh yes, there was this mad professor too,
Creating something that terrified
Our Auntie Betty.

Afterwards it took our family quite a time
To pull itself together,
But after six strong cups of cocoa
We finally recovered and voted it
The best film ever.

Islands in the River: Summer 1976

Day followed blazing day
And that summer seemed for ever;
Sweltering in school
We longed for the cool
Of the islands we'd found in the river.

And when school broke up we went there;
Said, "That's an end of the sun.
It's sure to rain
Till school starts again."
We were wrong – the gold days went on.

So we went to find the coolness,
Went where alders quiver,
Splashed through shallows
To the willows
On our islands in the river.

In low water three islands were one;
There Thomas and Ian and me
Now dug for treasure,
Now lazed at leisure,
Talked of floating away to the sea.

Ian was clever, knew books,
Was quick and dark and thin;
In stories spoke
Of river folk:
Ratty, Tom Sawyer, Huck Finn.

Camps we made and dens,
Laid plans to build a raft;
In the rushes
Sprang ambushes,
Fooled and fought and laughed.

Grubbed clay to seal a dam,
Caught tiddlers in the bays,
Terrified Tom
With a water-bomb:
Never such carefree days.

Not mentioned, hardly thought of,
Was next month when we'd part:
They'd move away,
Just me to stay –
A little sad at heart.

Long it was that summer;
Long but not for ever;
We went our ways
Remembering days
On islands in the river.

57 Varieties

It's a Heinz school ours;
If you want to know why it is
Well, we've got kids
In fifty-seven varieties:

'Cos we've got fighters
And lazy blighters,
Just a few posh kids,
Some not-enough-nosh kids,
Snotty kids, spotty kids,
A few really grotty kids,
First-in-the-queue kids,
Always-at-the-loo kids,

Scrappers, yappers,
Take a little nappers,
Nigglers, wrigglers,
Girlish gigglers,

26

Work-in-a-mess kids,
Couldn't-care-less kids,
Schemers, dreamers,
Playground screamers,
Fibbers, cribbers,
Poke you in the ribbers,
Sad kids, sunny kids,
Dad's-got-pots-of-money kids;

There's clumsy clots,
Swankpots, swots,
Teachers' pets
(The weedy wets!),
Just-look-at-me kids,
Wouldn't-hurt-a-flea kids,
Kids where the quiet is,
Kids where the riot is –
Just like I said:
Fifty-seven varieties . . .

If you think about that lot
It'll drive you up the wall;
If you ask me, it's a miracle
The place works at all.

Told Off

Not you again! You wretched pest!
Uh, here it comes; say nothing's best.

Why were you making such a din?
My dad could easy bash him in.

And yesterday you spilt that glue.
Mum'll tell him a thing or two.

It wasn't your fault, I suppose?
Coo, see the hairies up his nose!

Then there's the way you act in town . . .
Blimey, his specs are slipping down!

. . . Dressing like that – you're such a sight . . .
Wonder what's on TV tonight.

. . . Those sorry faces you put on.
Anyway, Maths is nearly gone.

A thorough pest! The worst I've seen!
You said that lot before, old bean.

A nuisance! You just can't be trusted!
Time for lunch. I hope there's custard.

You stand there dumb, without a thought . . .
Now that's what *you* think, dear old sport!

My Pal Pete

Pete's a pal of mine
But even I've got to admit
He is a little bit odd –
In fact, the word "eccentric"
Comes to mind.
Tell you what I mean:
The other day as usual
Pete was drinking his soup
Off his fork,
And when somebody asked him why,
He said, "Lasts longer like this, see."
And another thing:
He swats flies with a tennis racket –
"Gives 'em a sporting chance," Pete says.
And then he makes himself a drink
By putting coffee powder in a cup
And pouring tea on to it –
Calls it toffee.

A bit odd, as I say –
But he is a pal of mine.

We Hate You, Gordon Blue!

To borrow a saying from Dad:
"You know I'm not one to grouse,"
But just at the moment, as far as food goes,
Things are pretty hopeless at our house.
It all began when Mum decided
To do cookery at evening classes.
"Cookery, love?" says Dad,
Putting down the evening paper
And looking over his glasses.
"But everybody knows already, love,
You're the best cook in the universe;
Going to evening classes
Can only make you worse.
Besides, on the evenings you go
Who'll be getting my late teas?
What about my fish fingers and chips?
And my poached egg, pie and peas?"
And our kid and me –
Well, we had to agree,
'Cos who'd make the chocolate sauce
For our jelly?
Besides, if Mum went, we'd be left with Dad
And arguments about the telly:
He'd have us watching the wildlife
And travel programmes
And sitting in absolute silence,
Instead of watching the good stuff
Like Tarzan and horror and violence
All this didn't make
A blind bit of difference
Except to get Mum vexed –
She went muttering on about Women's Rights

And saying she might burn her bra next –
Though what that had to do
With cookery classes I never really saw.
Anyway, she goes, and in no time
She's rattling on to Mrs Uppercut next door
About how marvellous things are on
This Gordon Blue Cookery Course
And how they're doing these fancy dishes
Like roast hedgehog
With hazelnut sauce.
I suppose that's the name of the bloke in charge –
Funny name though: Gordon Blue,
But for Mum he's God, and take it from me
He's taught her a thing or two.

There isn't a chance in our house now
Of a favourite meal passing our lips –
I'm thinking of something like sausage,
Egg, beans, fried bread, black pudding
And chips.
Instead we get these high-class meals
With very funny names –
Like Cocko Van and Ratat Wee –
They sound more like party games.
We're there at the table last Friday
Thinking baked beans on toast
Would be nice,
When Mum breezes in with her latest creation:
Curried eggs and cucumber and rice.
And she chops these queer salads
She learned at her course –
Not lettuce, tomatoes and such –
But cabbage and apples, sultanas, bananas:
I can't say we care for them much.
Course, Dad does his best
To stick up for Mum:

31

He says with a bit of a laugh,
"Well love, I call that one
A real classy meal –
Much better than Ted's Transport Caff!"

But we long to get back
To the great meals of old:
Just fish and chips would be good,
Or liver and onions with mashies and mushies,
Or roast beef and Yorkshire pud.
But I reckon there's plenty of pain to come yet
Before Mum gets over her craze,
Things like anchovies, chili and curry and olives
And garlic that lingers for days.
I tell you this though: we're desperate men,
There may be something drastic to do;
So we're holding a meeting
To plan out a murder.
The victim is Gordon Blue.